BLACKBURN'S WEST END

This book is limited to 1000 copies.

No. _079_ of 1000.

BLACKBURN'S
WEST END

by

Matthew Cole

LANDY

Publishing

ISBN 1 872895 21 2

Landy Publishing have also published:-

Blackburn & Darwen A Century Ago by Alan Duckworth

Bits of Old Blackburn by J G Shaw & William Hulme, with drawings by Charles Haworth

The Blackburn Samaritan by Trevor Moore

Blackburn's Old Inns by George Miller

A Blackburn Miscellany edited by Bob Dobson

For details of these and other publications, contact

Landy Publishing
"Acorns"
3 Staining Rise
Staining
Blackpool FY3 0Bu
Tel/Fax: 01253 886103

Designed and produced by Coveropen Ltd. Tel: (0254) 425478

Printed and bound in Great Britain.

INTRODUCTION

CHANGE often inspires an interest in local history, and so it was with this book. when the groundwork for it was done, well over a decade ago, houses overlooking Beardwood from Lammack had recently been built, and a huge new motel stood at Yew Tree. Since then, further developments have swallowed up the last acre of that ground, and changed or obliterated many landmarks, both the familiar and the less well-known. Having watched this process as a local, I was motivated to look into the area's past as it moved on.

But the area of Blackburn beyond Corporation Park deserves attention for better reasons than idle or even sentimental curiosity (although these are no sins!): it was home to Blackburn's farmers, weavers and gentry, gateway to Preston and the coast, and finally gave splendid isolation to the town's leading citizens at the height of Blackburn's prosperity. The residents of this 'West End', which includes Billinge, Beardwood and Revidge, have always contributed to Blackburn life, and the evidence of that contribution remains with us. 'Blackburn's West End' tries to reflect that contribution, and perhaps renew some memories for those who know the area.

The names of those who have kindly helped with the preparation of the book – with interviews, documents or access to their homes – are legion, and I offer my most sincere thanks to them all. In particular, however, I should like to acknowledge the photography of George Bancroft, the advice of Barbara Riding and Robin Whalley, the assistance of staff at Blackburn Central Library, the generosity of those who allowed the reproduction of private photographs, and the Butcher family for their patient hospitality.

The story of Blackburn's West end is marked by the characteristic industry, creativity and personality of Blackburn people. I can only hope that it is told here with a semblance of the rigour and vitality with which it has been recounted to me!

MATTHEW COLE
JUNE 1994

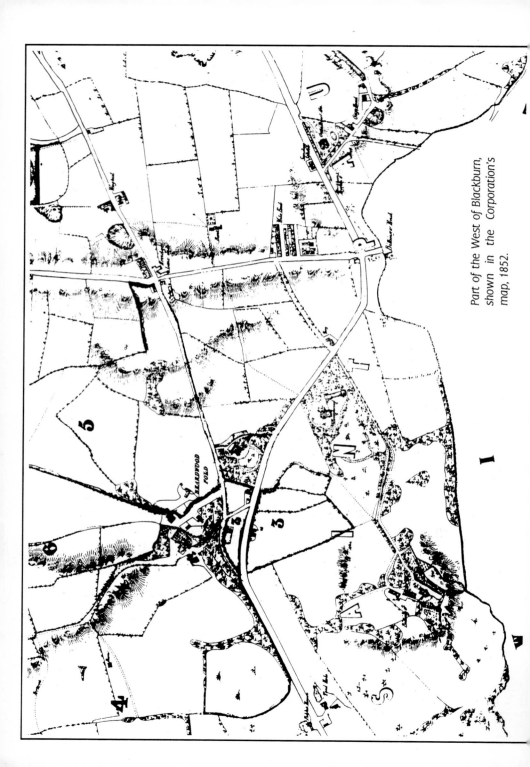

Part of the West of Blackburn, shown in the Corporation's map, 1852.

Origins & Early Days

PEOPLE have been farming the land West of Blackburn for nearly a thousand years – and probably more. The houses, records and even the very names their communities have left us reflect a history stretching back beyond the Norman Conquest.

Local place-names like 'Mellor', 'Billinge', 'Revidge' and 'Beardwood' are all forms of Old or Middle English terms telling of the shape or use of the land, and were first recorded in Lancashire in the Twelfth and Thirteenth Centuries. Mellor – from the Welsh 'Moelfre' or 'bare hill' – was first recognised in 1130 (then called Malver) and, as its name suggests, was probably less promising as farm land than the more marshy and sheltered tracts its inhabitants saw when looking towards Blackburn. It was there that a settlement was established whose name first appears at the Lancashire Inquests of 1258 as 'Berdewrthe' (later called 'Burdeswurth' or 'Burdeworthgreve', but thought to be the same place since known as Beardwood). The title is probably taken from the common Old English name 'Bearda', to whom belonged a 'worth', a homestead with enclosed land (although some have believed the name to be a mixture of Anglo-Saxon 'Beorh', meaning hill, and 'wudu', or wood). Similarly, Revidge probably combines a name (the Scandinavian 'Raef') with the Old English for 'ridge'. A glance at the telephone directory will show that Beardsworth and variants such as Beardsmore, Beardsley and Beardwood itself remain common as local surnames – there is also a Beardsworth Street at Brownhill.

The Lancashire Inquests heard that a Simon de Berdewrthe had been involved in a case about livestock-keeping in the Forest of Chippingdale, and other authorities mention Beardwood in 1296, 1305, 1311 and 1324. Arley Brook leading to Mellor is mentioned in the early Thirteenth Century, and Billinge (from the word 'bill', meaning 'sword') is identified as 'bovate' or pastoral land in 1212. Farm buildings dating back to the Seventeenth Century are still to be seen at Billinge Nook on Under Billinge Lane. Billinge Hill has been a landmark since May 1429, when the Court of Blackburn Hundred – a gathering of local lords governing the whole of North East Lancashire – met on the hilltop.

The Old Road and its Neighbourhood

THESE communities were built around one of Blackburn's oldest roads, the route from Preston and the Ribble into the town itself. It passed Samlesbury's Fourteenth-Century Great Hall, which acquired its West wing, chapel and archery field in the Fifteenth; it proceeded past Mellor, through Toad Hole and Beardwood, and over the Brow. Descending into Blackburn from Revidge, the old road went via two of the town's oldest properties: Gawthorpe farm and spring, (now lost) and Bank House still standing lower down Duke's Brow. This is the famous Jacobean home of the 'Duke o' th' Bank' – a nickname adopted by its occupant in the Seventeenth Century – to which Sir Gilbert Houghton marched his Royalist troops and cannon to fire upon Blackburn on Christmas Eve, 1642. From there the route passed down what it now Montague Street to Snig Brook and into town. This thoroughfare must have carried its fair share of Blackburn's traffic from the town's earliest days onwards, and though largely obliterated by later developments, its original path is still distinct as it veers from Preston New Road near Mellor and Samlesbury Green, and ploughing straight on where Beardwood Brow turns sharply at its base. Until recent times this portion of disused road was still a well-maintained and hedged pathway, "from which", Blackburn historian William Abram recalled at the end of the

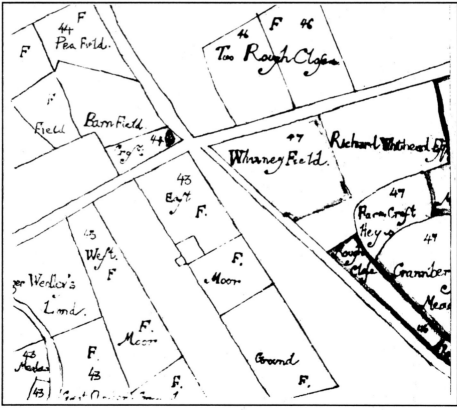

Lang's map of Blackburn (1739) shows the crossroads where Duke's Brow, rising from the bottom right, meets Revidge.

Nineteenth Century, *"a notion may be formed of its pristine character"*. Today the route is barely distinguishable, too overgrown and eroded even for pedestrians.

Other remnants of Beardwood's pre-industrial past are still visible in the homes and workplaces of the settlement's residents of three or four hundred years ago. Whilst, like most of their contemporaries, they were farmers, this was not the only string to the family bow, as Blackburn's Vicar, Thomas Starkie, wrote in 1807:

"Little can be said on behalf of the state of agriculture in this parish. Estates are generally divided into small farms, for the purpose of supplying the farmer, who is generally a weaver, with milk and butter for his family. It is by the loom chiefly that rents are paid."

The Seventeenth-and Eighteenth Century houses at Billinge End, Mile End and at the top of Beardwood Brow share with those they overlook in Beardwood the signs of homes in which children carded wool or cotton, women spun, and men operated the handloom before selling their wares to local merchants or 'putters-out'. Indeed, as late as 1841, the census showed only 18 farmers, but 383 weavers, in this area of Blackburn.

Farm buildings are the oldest ones in Beardwood: one particular cavernous barn, recently converted into a four-bedroomed house, dates from 1620. The oldest cottages in Beardwood Fold originally date from 1640 and 1673, and still bear classic features of weavers' cottages of the time, such as their substantial lintels and long windows to let in light. Still in use as a farm until recently, Beardwood Cottage has served a variety of functions, including accommodating the Thwaites family's laundry house. In the 1840s, these buildings included a beer-shop. Other houses in the Fold are in Eighteenth-Century style, and were also used as weavers' cottages. Across Beardwood Brow stands a restored property beside Preston New Road which once housed Lodge's Nurseries, and until recent years also exhibited a hayloft of mud, clay and branches. It had a loom cavity in its wall, telling of an earlier age. Now divided from this property by a Nineteenth-Century highway is 491 Preston New Road, a farm and coach-house built in 1797 which once boasted a hayloft, barn, pig-sties and dairy. It also acted as a local pub. This portion of land was known as Higher Toad Hole, and though the driver's quarters above the coach-house were lost earlier this century, the building still gives a sense of the increasingly substantial property being invested in Beardwood.

Buildings of the Seventeenth Century still stand at Toad Hole further down Preston New Road. Labourers' cottages and a barn there, recently converted to modern housing, were once set in a copse with further outbuildings, a large pond and a right of way leading to where Wyfordby Avenue now stands. Arley Brook was the cause of regular flooding for the tenants in those days. In living memory, the buildings still at Toad Hole retained loom cavities and other signs of the weaving and farming lifestyle which dominated the area.

Local People

WE also know something of the people themselves who lived and worked in the Beardwood area. Blackburn's parish registers of the Seventeenth Century gives an account of the births, burials and marriages in as many as twelve families resident for several generations in the houses and cottages to the West of the town.

Amongst the larger groups were the Whalley family, the Pickups and the Duckworths. Other names still familiar in East Lancashire were the Dewhursts of Billinge Scar, and at Toad Hole, the Whaley family and the Claytons. The Dewhurst family were of yeoman stock (attendants to officials in the nobility) and had owned the estate of *Billins Carr* since the reign of Queen Elizabeth I. its original name – it was also known as *Beardwood Green* and *Little Beardwood* – means '*marsh*', and is remembered in *Carr Lane* leading to the surviving Eighteenth-Century *Little Billinge Scar Farm* above the estate. Its owner at the time was William Dewhurst, who was nominated a governor of Blackburn Grammar School when the Queen granted its charter in 1567. Residents of the area such as the Dewhursts and the Gillibrands of Beardwood were supporters of the school in the Sixteenth and Seventeenth Centuries. Throughout the Eighteenth its governors included the Shuttleworths of Gawthorpe on Duke's Brow. The pattern was taken up in more recent times by others such as the Sudells and Thwaites who came to live in the area. After 1584 Dewhurst let part of the land out, but later passed the deeds on to his son John. When Blackburn's waste lands were enclosed by Commissioners in 1618, John was awarded 17 acres of this "improved land" on Revidge Moor to accompany the Billinge property. These were surrendered in 1645 when John married Jane Snaipe of Blackburn (in exchange for a £90 dowry from Jane's father), an exchange witnessed by Beardwood residents John and Roger Gillibrand. By this time, the property included a house and over 24 acres of land as well as the converted waste. Other documents of the time mention a barn, stables, pig-sties and gardens. At the end of the Seventeenth Century, Billinge Scar was sold to Edward Dewhurst for £358, and remained in the family (at one time in trust because the heir was only 15) until 1770, when it was sold for £1,200.

The names listed in the parish register at Beardwood itself were in all probability the residents of the homes of the period still to be found there. In a perhaps more roomy property (most likely a forerunner of Beardwood Old Hall) would have lived the Haworth family, whose head Laurence Haworth, (1623-75) is listed in Blackburn Parish Register from 1656 as a '*Gentleman*', and whose family at Higher Croft could trace their pedigree back to the reign of Henry III. Though the title of Gentleman was losing formal meaning by Laurence's time, it still denoted ownership of land run by local tenant farmers or bailiffs, a coat of arms and even a lifestyle of occasional hunting or business trips to major towns and cities when most never left their parish. Haworth, for example, was entrusted with the Billinge Scarr estate after John Dewhurst's marriage in 1645, and was also probably related to the Laurence Haworth who became a governor of the Grammar School in 1662. At any rate, Haworth's title lent a sense of independent existence to Beardwood, granted the status of 'township' in church registers at the baptism of his daughter, Ann, in 1666. Such Baptisms were for the Howarth family carried out at home rather than in Blackburn. This may bear testimony either to their good relations with the clergy, or to their concern for the health of their infants, five of whom died during the first half of the 1650s. One son, Thomas, took Laurence's title in Beardwood, and survived until 1694.

As the industrial revolution dawned, with all its implications for Blackburn, the land to the town's West already had a long history. It was a stable community linked to Preston, Samlesbury, Mellor and Blackburn itself, and was recognised in contemporary maps, legal documents and church records. In the Beardwood area, some hundred or more people worked their land and looms, and watched as occasionally new farms or homes were added to the small stock of isolated cottages. What was to come escalated that change with a speed which reflected the growth of Blackburn in dramatic scale and style.

The Coat of Arms of Laurence Haworth of Beardwood (1623-75)

The Impact of Industry

THE march of industrial Blackburn towards its Western fields took a very literal form early on in the process. In 1818, six thousand workers in the mills of Henry Sudell marched from Blakey Moor to his home at Woodfold Hall, on the far side of Billinge Hill, to demand a five per cent pay rise on account of the severe effects of the trade depression. The journey was challenging politically as much as physically, for whilst the four-or-five- mile jaunt on the rough roads over Revidge and on to the Hall was little more than a brisk walk in the days before modern transport (even for the hungry), such combined action by workers was still illegal and risked transportation or death for its leaders. Sudell, however, was a millionaire magnate who could afford munificence – he granted the rise knowing that his domination of the trade would force other employers to follow suit.

Sudell was the first of a series of industrialists and dignitaries who chose the West of Blackburn as the location for spectacular new residences which put the produce of their workers' labour to use in providing them with both comfort and glory. Beardwood and Billinge became the shop window of Blackburn's manufacturing and municipal leadership.

Sudell's home at Woodfold Hall is perhaps the best example of all. Built in 1798 from stone quarried at Abbot's Brow in Mellor, this was a vast and imposing neo-classical construction set in 400 acres of landscaped grounds stocked with deer and wildfowl, and surrounded by a four-mile-long wall nine feet high. Sudell's prosperity was reflected in his patronage of less fortunate Mellor folk, his contribution to the site and building of St. John's Church in Blackburn (the tower of which bears a weather vane in the form of a loom and shuttle in his memory) and in his lifestyle of foxhunting at Alum Scar, where deer-rings and an icehouse for game can still be seen. It was from there that he would ride into town by way of Billinge, Revidge and Duke's Brow in a coach and four flanked by postilions in crimson and gold, and lined by employees with caps deferentially doffed. *"His entry into Blackburn"* George Miller later wrote, *"was almost a state occasion"*

Sudell fled Woodfold when bankrupted through unwise foreign investments in 1827. The Hall was briefly the residence of John Fowden Hindle, High Sheriff of the County, who would hold breakfast functions for "numerous and fashionable parties" in the gardens, entertained by bands, before departing for the Assizes at Lancaster accompanied by a retinue of officials, trumpeters and javelin men. After 1849, Woodfold was purchased by the Thwaites through a family connection, and became one of several of their properties in the West of Blackburn. They and their descendents developed the estate of some 68 farms, spending considerable sums on it and their lands in Mellor. Its stables produced prize-winning horses, its interior was altered to create a huge sealed atrium known as

WOODFOLD HALL

'The Justice Room' in which business was conducted, and locals even recited a poem comparing the windows to the days of the year! It remained in use until 1949, when it was left derelict. Yet, though its builder was gone, Woodfold set the tone for the development of the Beardwood area between the hall and Blackburn itself. The agricultural settlement became the roost of the town's wealthy and famous, who were keen to stay close enough to watch over their mills and breweries, but far enough away for comfort.

In Beardwood Fold itself, this process began modestly enough: the turn of the Nineteenth Century saw the building of Beardwood Old Hall in its present Regency Gothic form, dating from 1830; new cottages and farm buildings were also springing up, and existing ones were undergoing a sort of mild gentrification – the two weavers' cottages which made up what is now Beardwood Lodge, for example, acquired a bordered garden graced by carefully-planted poplars. To these more modern and exclusively residential properties moved the professionals and small businessmen of flourishing Blackburn: by the 1840s and '50s these included Dr. William Forest, who lived at No. 9 Beardwood Fold, but had rooms in St. John's Place, as did Richard Barton Dodgson, who lived at No. 6; William Barlow Fairbrother at No. 13 also owned houses in King Street and Montague Street; and others living on Revidge kept properties in Wensley Fold, Fish Lane (now Cardwell Place) and, in the case of Ben Sandford, had shops at four addresses in Fleming Square. The properties these men owned in the West of Blackburn were their escape from work, where they entertained guests and were served by their own domestic staff.

The Effects of the Turnpike

THE immediate cause of much of this development was the renewed contact with Blackburn town centre brought about by the opening of Preston New Road in 1826. The project was amongst the later of a flood of turnpike roads built between the 1750s and the 1830s to meet the demands of industrial production and trade. Prior to this time, many roads had changed little since Roman times, and were maintained by voluntary subscription or statute labour – public service work carried out by all adults, rather like jury service today. As a result they could be steep or winding, dusty in Summer, impassable in Winter – and no match for the heavy traffic imposed by Blackburn's industrial growth.

Turnpike roads were paid for by developers who would buy rights over a route at auction, and recover their building costs by imposing charges on travellers. It was first decided that surveyors should stake out the route of Preston New Road in September 1824, when the first lot, running through Beardwood and Toad Hole, was bought by David, Daniel and William Duckworth for £150. The work was hampered by the watery conditons there, and the Duckworths discovered that the names of

Billinge Carr, Spout Fold (behind Billinge Scar) and Toad Hole were no accidents! The contract required the builders to divert Arley Brook through a culvert, and cover the water course with a drain, and the road's gradient was to be as gentle as possible. In October 1825, the Duckworths were reprimanded by the surveyors for failing properly to fill up a hollow at Toad Hole for this purpose.

As the new route to Preston and the West coast, the turnpike must have taken considerable traffic. In 1834 it was remeasured for milestones, one of which went at Shackerley Brook in Toad Hole, and which eight years later became the site of a new toll bar for collecting charges, replacing those at Mire Ash and Duke's Brow, and a smaller side bar at Billinge End. Investors such as the Duckworths were eager to at least recoup costs they had incurred bidding for lots at auction and (they claimed) maintaining the road, and often imposed controversial charges, which in some parts of the country led to riots. A more common and less dramatic dispute occurred at the Shackerley bar in 1866, when funeral contractor John Dixon, who worked from the George Inn in Darwen Street, refused to pay. Those travelling to burials and church services were exempt from charges, but Mr. Dixon – later Councillor, then Alderman Dixon as a member of Blackburn Borough Council for Park ward – was summonsed after it was discovered that his carriage was without any load!

In 1890, such proceedings came to an end when the turnpike and keeper's cottage alongside it were pulled down as the road became County Council

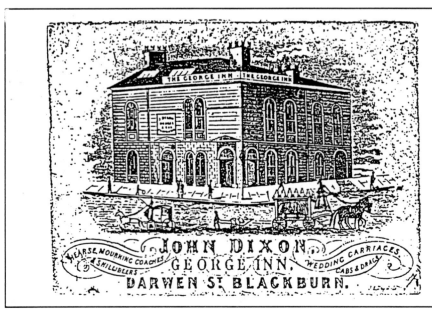

The calling card of Councillor Dixon, whose hearse slipped through the Shackerley Toll.

property and was declared *"free to the public forever"*. Local MP and former Mayor of Blackburn William Coddington, who lived near Beardwood at Wycollar, was determined to be both the last to pay a toll, and the first to pass through Shackerly bar free of charge. He therefore waited by the keeper's cottage in his carriage until just before the tolls expired at midnight on October 31st, paying to travel out of town, and passing back free just after the clock struck twelve to stake yet another claim to a place in Blackburn's history. It was only afterwards that his boast was disputed discreetly to friends by his coachman, who had pipped him at the post on the return journey!

One by-product of the new road which was a familiar sight to local residents until recently was the Yew Tree Inn. This substanial brick building was a welcome sight to travellers from the second quarter of the nineteenth century onwards, and as early as 1839 was the starting point for Blackburn's first annual steeplechase, an event drawing thousands of spectators. The Inn's motley clientele of travellers gave it a chequered history, and on Good Friday of 1885, Joseph Eddleston, a 52-year old labourer from Hancock Street was beaten to death outside the Yew Tree in full sight of the landlord. James Bailey, a weaver, of Isherwood Street was promptly convicted of manslaughter by a Blackburn jury.

Initially run as a farm by the Pollitt family who already worked the land at Toad Hole, but later becoming a full-fledged public house under Robert Pollitt, the Yew Tree was taken over by the Thwaites family in 1888, until which time its tenants were listed in local directories as both farmers and publicans. The farmland and outbuildings attached to the pub were worked until the Second World War, and the remains of a well used as a back-up to the pumped water supply can still be seen beside Preston New Road. Pints flowed from the Inn's pumps until 1972, when, after the establishment of the Saxon Inn (now Moat House) Motel, it was used as staff accommodation only. In 1984 the building was pulled down, and only its carved stone sign remains at the side of the road in Toad Hole.

Blackburn's Stately Homes

NEARER into Blackburn, however the new road brought with it the first signs of more palatial residences. Within two years of the road's opening, work had begun on *Beardwood Mansion*, the grounds of which covered the six-acre site now occupied by Beardwood Drive between Beardwood Brow and the main road in town. This was the first of a new generation of homes which marked a stark contrast with those already in place in the area: its long and sweeping driveway led through landscaped gardens on the steep terrain looking out towards the West. Around the main building stood a coach-house, stables, summer-house, potting house, kitchen garden, drying-ground, shippon barn and a well.

For most of the Nineteenth Century its occupant was Henry Hargreaves, a Blackburn solicitor with offices in fashionable King Street and Clayton Street, who outdid any of his neighbours in 1840s Beardwood with a housekeeper, four servants, a coachman and his wife all 'living in', along with his own spouse and daughter. Whilst the servants and coachman's family had their separate cottages on the estate, Hargreaves had the use of the eighteen rooms in the main house. He remained at Beardwood until his ninetieth year, but after four decades, his generation gave way to a still more prestigious class of resident.

Most famous of the residents at Beardwood mansion was Sir John Rutherford. Educated at the Lower Bank Academy (which still stands at the foot of Duke's Brow) in the 1860s, he became a Colonel commanding the Duke of Lancaster's Own Yeomanry, inherited his father's partnership in Shaw's brewery in the Salford area of Blackburn, and became Mayor of Blackburn at the age of 34 in 1888. Plain John Rutherford until he received a baronetcy in 1916, he moved into Beardwood during his twenty- seven year stint as MP for Darwen at the turn of the century. First elected in 1895, he retrieved for the Conservatives the seat lost to the Liberals three years earlier by the Prime Minister's son, Viscount Cranborne: after a close-fought contest as a keen Unionist, he was given a hostile reception by Irish Nationalists in the Stoney Flatts district, where – despite being accompanied by a member of *"the fairer sex"* – his victory parade was reported to have been pelted with sticks and stones! He fought seven elections and won six, only being absent from the House between the two contests of 1910. Sir John was President of Blackburn Royal Infirmary, and like his father, was a J.P., both in Blackburn and in Dumfrieshire. Of Scottish descent, he maintained a home at Rutherford Lodge in Roxboroughshire as well as Beardwood.

Apart from his life in politics, Sir John also played in the early line-up of Blackburn Rovers, (whose ground at the time was to be found on Dukes Brow near what is now Granville Road) cultivated orchids with the help of three gardeners in the large conservatory which was built alongside the mansion, and after retiring from the Commons, became famous on the turf as the owner of *'Solario'*, the colt which won his first classic race, the 1925 St. Leger, and the 1926 Coronation Cup at Epsom. Despite an offer of £100,000 (between two and three million pounds at today's prices) from the Aga Khan, Sir John declined to part with such a prized steed.

Within four years of Sir John's death (in 1932) the mansion and its lands, extending to the brook through Beardwood, were sold to Walter Duckworth for less than £3,000 and demolished to make way for the *'garden city'* homes now in its place. Only the garage was spared the hammer, and stood untouched until recently, when it was refashioned as part of a modern home on Beardwood Brow, and can still be recognised surrounded by traces of the former cobbled yard in which it stood.

Part of the land around Sir John's home was given over to building the home of a fellow parliamentarian and former Mayor of Blackburn, Sir William Coddington, Bart. Eldest son in one of Blackburn's leading mill-owning families (his uncle was John Hopwood, Conservative MP for Clitheroe) and its Conservative MP from 1880 onwards, Sir William inherited 'Wycollar' (also commonly known as *Coddington Hall*) next door to Rutherford's home, while it was still being built, on his father's death in 1867. Though he maintained another address at Grosvenor Square, London, 'Wycollar' was his home from the 1870s until his death in 1918. Four years later 'Wycollar' became the home of textile manufacturer Jack Eddleston, who sold the estate for demolition when business hit hard times in 1930. Its only visible remains are the lodge house on Preston New Road, the estate walls along Wycollar Road, White Road and Beardwood Brow, and 'York House', built on the high slopes of the gardens for Jack's son, Robert.

Across the road another mansion, known as 'Beardwood Hall', had been erected by the 1840s. A graceful building, with a separate cottage for three servants, it served as the home of a string of well-known Blackburn families, including the Astleys, who retired to Beardwood in the 1880s after success in the grocery and textile businesses, and stayed until after the turn of the century, when J. J. L. Irving – a descendant of the inventor Crompton, and of Blackburn's first mill owner – moved in. In the 1930s, the Hall passed into the hands of another cotton family, led by Sir John Taylor, and was finally a family home for the Woolleys of Cupal Pharmaceuticals. In the late 1950s, when it was turned over to its present use as a hospital, living rooms downstairs became wards for the elderly; upstairs quarters were used for consultations. Originally opened as 'Our Lady of Compassion Hospital', it has since been substantially extended, and gone into entirely private hands as 'Beardwood Hospital'.

Other Blackburn dignitaries living in the area by the late Nineteenth Century included W.H. ('Harry') Hornby, Sir William Coddington's colleague as Blackburn's other Tory MP from 1886, whose father and brother had also held the seat before him. He lived at 'Whinfield' near Billinge End in the 1890s. His neighbours included a clutch of cotton dealers, manufacturers and Justices of the Peace such as the Thompsons at 'Beardwood Cliff' (now 'Nazareth House'); James Dickinson and Eli Heyworth, both of whom owned 'Whinfield'; and members of the Thwaites family. It was the presence of this last, and most influential, clan which brought the area its most prestigious and grandiose residences.

The Thwaites family had moved out of their original home in Cleaver Street adjacent to the Eanam brewery by the middle of the Nineteenth Century, when they lived in East Park Road, and later at 'West Bank' in Preston New Road. When John Thwaites retired to leave brother Daniel in charge, however, he became the first to move to greater seclusion further out of town. In 1856 he took up residence in a new property at 'Troy' on Preston New Road. The name had previously been given to the land between Mile End on Revidge and the turnpike road, which was worked by a local gardener and farm labourers. Now it was taken for a huge house with ornamental gardens built across Preston New

*Mr. W. H. Hornby—C.... 9,265
*Mr. W. Coddington—C.... 9,046

Mr. John Taylor—L 7,272
Mr. J. Heyworth—L...........6,694
Conservative majority ...——1,774
Electorate: 17,661.

1885 poll: Coddington (C), 9,168; Peel (C), 8,425; Briggs (L), 6,739; Boothman (L), 5,341—Conservative majority (on aggregate vote), 2,756—unopposed.

1886: Coddington (C), and Hornby (C) unopposed.

Mr. William Coddington, who has been Mayor of Blackburn, is the head of a large firm of cotton spinners and a manufacturer, and is a much better printseller than a politician. He is a thoroughgoing party man, voting strictly according to orders. He has never ventured to address the House, and even in his native town finds some difficulty in stringing together the regulation political platitudes. He is a director of the Midland Railway, and is 63.
43, Grosvenor-square, W.; Wycollar, Blackburn. Junior Carlton.

MR. W. CODDINGTON

Mr. William Henry Hornby is a Tory by birth and breeding. His father represented Blackburn for many years, and his brother followed when his father retired to his Cheshire retreat. The Hornbys have long been connected with the borough, and own large cotton mills, in which they employ hundreds of workmen. But the muscles of the Hornbys have done even better work than their brains. The Lancastrians are ardent admirers of sport in all its branches, and Blackburn would return their pet half-back to St. Stephen's (if he would go) rather than the greatest statesman who ever breathed. Mr. Briggs

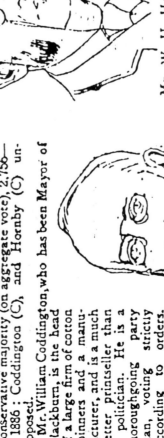

MR. W. H. HORNBY.

owed much of his popularity to his brother's greyhounds. So the Hornbys are popular because of their brother's fame in the cricket field. Mr. A. N. Hornby would be at the head of any poll that was ever taken in Blackburn. Mr. W. H. Hornby, who was first returned for the borough in 1886, is a county alderman and a director of the Lancashire and Yorkshire Railway Company. He married a niece of the late Bishop of Winchester, and is 51.
Whinfield, Blackburn. Carlton.

Road, where John Thwaites lived for the next three decades. His family remained there until the 1920s, and after the Second World War the building was taken over as part of Blakey Moor Central School. In the 1960s it was finally demolished to erect the more modern premises of Beardwood (formerly Billinge) School which stands there today. However, it was John's younger brother Daniel who made an even bigger impact on the area.

Mr. JOHN RUTHERFORD, D.L., J.P., M.P. for the Darwen Division of Lancashire

John Rutherford, M.P., D.L., J.P., Beardwood, Blackburn, Summerhill, Annan, N.B., and 101, Mount Street, London, W.; son of the late John Rutherford, J.P.,; born at Blackburn, in 1854; educated at the Royal Grammar School, Lancaster, and Glasgow University. Member of Parliament for the Darwen Division of Lancashire since 1895; Mayor of Blackburn, 1888-89; Hon. Colonel in the Duke of Lancaster's Own Yeomanry Cavalry; a Governor of the Cotton District Convalescent Fund. Clubs: Carlton, Bootle's, and Cavalry.

Irving. — JAMES JOHN LANCASTER IRVING, Beardwood Hall, Blackburn; son of William Irving, M.D., J.P. for the County of Lancaster; born at Blackburn, June 27th, 1855: educated at Windermere College. Interested in art, also in agricultural pursuits, and has been greatly successful in the Royal Agricultural and County Shows; Conservative in politics; member of the Church of England. He is, through his mother, a direct descendant of Samuel Crompton, the celebrated inventor of the spinning mill. His grandfather erected, in 1776-77, the first cotton spinning mill ever built in Blackburn.

Two of the Beardwood gentry recognised in W.B. Thompson's 'Lancashire at the Opening of the Twentieth Century'.

Opposite: *This report of the results of the 1892 General Election shows that Blackburn's West End had returned both of the town's M.P.'s.*

The Birth of 'Billinge Scar'

FOLLOWING John, the shrewd and highly successful millionaire brewer Daniel Thwaites made his own home in 1858 on the site of a sandstone quarry further down Preston New Road. Known later as *'Nazareth House'*, Thwaites called it *'Beardwood Cliff'*, and lived there for nearly twenty years. The house was set in spacious, carefully-laid gardens with fountains and tennis-courts, and several outbuildings including large greenhouses and the lodge house which is still visible from the road; the elegant interior boasted ornate plaster work, magnificent marble fireplaces and a billiard-room.

Thwaites married in 1859, and with the birth of daughter Elma Amy (later Mrs. Yerburgh) in 1864 and his entry into public life in 1875 as another of Blackburn's Tory MPs, he decided to move on. *'Beardwood Cliff'* was handed over to other members of his family, and then sold to cotton dealers the Thompsons, before the Nazarene Sisters moved there from St. Alban's Place in 1914. The stables and garage became classrooms and dormitories, and two rooms in the house were converted into a chapel. The home was supported by voluntary contributions collected by the Sisters in Blackburn. Orphaned and deprived children were taught in Nazareth House until the Second World War, but since then it has operated exclusively as a home for the elderly. Thwaites' original building survived until 1988, when it was pulled down to make way for more suitable accommodation for its occupants. Only its datestone and outbuildings remain to be seen today.

On leaving *'Beardwood Cliff'*, Daniel Thwaites had embarked on a still more ambitious project at *'Billinge Scar'*. Since passing out of the hands of the Dewhurst family in the 1770s, the land and buildings there had been owned and occupied by a variety of clergy, yeomen and gentry – latterly attorney Henry Brock Hollinshead, formerly of Hollinshead Hall estate in Tockholes. The property which accommodated Hollinshead, his wife, three children and four servants was regarded as *"old fashioned, rather quaint, but not of large dimensions"* when Thwaites took it over, and in 1876 plans were drawn up of what was, with rather implausible modesty, called an *"extension"* of the existing buildings.

Daniel Thwaites' home at Billinge Scar was impressive by most standards – and certainly by comparison with the conditions of those who worked for, or even lived near him. Set in five acres of walled gardens planned under Mrs. Thwaites' instruction, where the household grew their fruits, it was a four-floor, thirty-four room structure incorporating twelve bedrooms, (half of which were for domestic staff) a wine cellar, library and school room for Elma. A coachman's quarters and stables at the rear of the house formed a courtyard which, together with the Elizabethan-style stone frontage, transomed, mullioned and hood moulded windows, and the embattled roofline of an imposing tower, gave the impression of aristocratic rural retreat which so many manufacturers were eager to recreate. Here he lived out his retirement from public life after defeat in the 1880 election.

Upon Elma's marriage to barrister Robert Armstrong Yerburgh, MP for Chester, in 1888, Daniel moved out of 'Billinge Scar' and to his retreat in Scotland, only to die within a matter of weeks. The Yerburghs added to the house a conservatory between the drawing and dining rooms. Mr. Howson, Thwaites' steward, was responsible for the grounds as well as for this considerable extension, which took three years and housed tree ferns, palms, creeping and flowering plants, along with marble statues symbolising the four seasons. The interior was walled with mirrors, and lit by globes of white ground glass, using both gas and electricity.

In 1895, Robert and Elma Yerburgh moved to Henry Sudell's former home at 'Woodfold Hall'. 'Billinge Scar' waited more than a decade before being taken over by cotton magnate William Birtwistle, the man reputed in his time to command more looms than any other individual in the world. Birtwistle fitted the lifestyle of Blackburn's Edwardian West End perfectly – the owner of large yachts and several motor cars (in fact he was the first to hold a driving licence in Blackburn) and a relative by blood or marriage of the town's great and good, including the Astleys of 'Beardwood Hall', the Eddlestons of 'Wycollar', and a twelve-strong branch of the Birtwistle family at 'Springfield', further up Preston

A drawing of Billinge Scar in the 1890's, showing the newly-constructed conservatory on the left of the main building.

New Road. His older brother Richard – a director of Roe Lee Mills – had even scored Blackburn Rovers' first goal in their 1884 F.A. Cup victory.

When William Birtwistle left 'Billinge Scar' in 1921, the house was passed on to his son, Brigadier-General Arthur Birtwistle, who, in addition to his duties as chairman or director of a string of companies including Hawkins' Printers, was a J.P. and Deputy-Lieutenant of Lancashire. Although he never entered public political life in the same way as his neighbours, Arthur Birtwistle earned a reputation for genuine concern about the fortunes of his workers and others in times of hardship. He secured from his father 22 acres of land at Balderstone to establish allotments for unemployed men, and deliberately recruited domestic staff from areas worst hit by depression as far away as County Durham. An annual 'field day' was held at 'Billinge Scar' for pupils who marched there ceremonially from Blackburn's Ragged School. 'Billinge Scar's' eight full- time servants (fitted with a series of uniforms for different occasions), as well as the regular parties of guests whom Birtwistle entertained, were given access to the full facilities of the estate, which included tennis courts, an 80-foot swimming pool and even a wendy house built in the garden for Birtwistle's daughter Violet. Surviving employees still testify to the General's character as *"a perfect gentleman"*, echoing the feelings of one in his command during the Great War who declared: *"I would follow that man wherever he asked me to go, and I shall salute him whenever I meet him as long as I live"*.

The General died at 'Billinge Scar' in May 1937, and the property's auction was described as *"a unique opportunity of acquiring a charming and picturesque mansion as a gentleman's residence"*. It included a ballroom, a sun lounge made from Thwaites' conservatory with an Italian mosaic floor valued at £2,500, seven greenhouses (one, 150 feet in length, with vines), garage space for six cars complete with an inspection pit, and grounds tended by eight gardeners. Although plans were made to put the buildings to use as a gentlemen's club or a training establishment for telephone engineers, the building suffered from dry rot, and could find no buyers in days of decline for the cotton industry and its giants like Birtwistle. It was requisitioned by various ministries during the war, and eventually sold by Birtwistle's widow in 1945 to a Leigh businessman, who waited only two years before turning it over to a Blackpool demolition team, eager for building materials amid a post-war shortage.

The catalogue of materials recovered from the demolition is in itself a bizarre tribute to the former ostentatious elegance of the ruin. It took three years to pull down nine-tenths of the structure, (including the original house which formed the core of Thwaites' construction) leaving only the coach-house which still stands. Amongst other remains, the demolition team took away 3,000 handmade bricks, 100 tons of lead, vast quantities of timber and glass, and 2,500 tons of dressed Italian stone. 60 tons of girders were retrieved from the swimming-pool roof alone. Tons of high quality masonry lay as rubble across the gardens, littering the fountains – simply too great a challenge for the asset-strippers – surrounded only by the remaining – and deteriorating – wall. One of Blackburn Borough's grandest showpieces had collapsed into ugly indignity as spectacularly as it had arisen.

As with so many aspects of Blackburn's history, its West end changed and changed again dramatically with the rise and decline of King Cotton. The residential directories of the stretch of Preston New Road from Billinge End to Toad Hole at the turn of the century read like a Who's Who of the town's political and industrial communities: a grouping of wealthy and powerful men who shared not only their address in Blackburn and their commercial interests there, but also their influence through the magistracy, their support of the Rovers and the East Lancs Cricket Club, and their Parliamentary careers, homes in West London and social life at the Carlton Club. These were figures of national influence, but with a fierce local pride – so much that some, like Coddington and Hornby, never even lowered themselves to speak in the Commons, whilst others like Thwaites concentrated on parochial interests such as campaigning for an end to duties on cotton goods exported to India. Other powerful local figures included Thomas Ritzemer, the founder of the Evening Telegraph, who built and lived at 'Quarry Glen', Billinge End, during the 1920s. He had contested Blackburn as a Liberal Parliamentary candidate against his neighbours, Coddington and Hornby, but was unsuccessful as an 'outsider' with less than ten years in the town to his name. In a hundred years, the West of Blackburn had gone from spinning and weaving in farm cottages to politicking amongst the employers of the town's great textile firms. Yet theirs was an era nearing its end, and the last resident of the area to enter Parliament symbolised the coming age. Whilst Edwardian capitalists enjoyed their comfortable surroundings in Beardwood, Philip Snowdon, Blackburn's Labour MP from 1906-18 (and Labour's first Chancellor of the Exchequer) lived in more modest circumstances at 2, Leopold Road, Duke's Brow. As the terraces of respectable workers spread over Revidge, the opulent social and physical world of Victorian capital retreated and collapsed: this was to be the story of the next century.

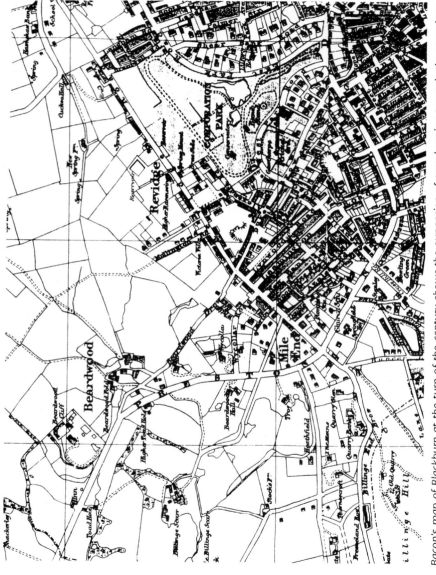

Bacon's map of Blackburn at the turn of the century shows the expansion of new housing towards the mansions which still stood around Beardwood.

Into Living Memory

THE changes which were to occur in the West of Blackburn during the Twentieth century could be seen approaching, almost military- style, over the brow of Revidge at the end of the Nineteenth.

The steep terrain from the top of Montague Street to Beardwood was, in the 1850s, still mostly open ground, punctuated only by quarries at Limefield, Wagtail and Billinge End, individual homes such as *Bank House* and *Oozehead House*, and farms or cottages forming isolated colonies with their own identities. Wagtail, on the upper slopes of Duke's Brow, and Pinchem (where the *West View* pub now stands) elected their own Mayors, who even conducted exchange visits! The beer-house run at *New Bank* farm in the 1830s, out of easy reach of the Blackburn authorities, was notorious for dog-racing, cock-fighting, and what were politely reported as *"some wild characters' revels at week-ends"*. The 1851 census returns show over fifty addresses at Mile End, including those of hand- and power-loom weavers, a carter, coal dealer, charwoman, bike-maker, and a rural police constable. A further ten families lived at Wagtail. Local recreations included football at the site on Granville Road later used by the Rovers, (in which unruly games at least one man suffered a broken leg) hunting at *Fox Delph*, a marl-pit in which an animal had been chased to death behind where the *Fox and Grapes* pub stands, and walks on the right of way from *Bank House* to Shear Brow before the Park was opened. This path – known as '*The Grammar School Back*' – still cuts through the grounds of Queen Elizabeth's, and was said a century and a half ago to be haunted by the boggart of an unfortunate local who had suffocated there one cold winter's night. This area, which sheltered the dignitaries in Beardwood from the conditions of the town, still had a very distinctive flavour of its own.

New Villas and Terraces

THIS was all to change in the coming hundred years. The homes of the wealthy industrialists who had sought solitude in the area were to be surrounded and then supplanted by those of their managers and even their workmen – the housing which remains there today. The process began with the creation of Corporation Park in lands bought from Joseph Feilden in 1855, which turned *Pemberton Clough* and its old reservoir into fifty acres of landscaped gardens, carriageways and ornamental lakes (paid for by Mayor William Pilkington), overlooked by the Russian cannon captured at Sebastopol, and surrounded by two new roads linking the Park gates with Revidge. Thousands attended the grand opening, at which the London Illustrated Times reported *"a procession entered the park amid salvos of artillery which contributed to do* honour to the occasion and to alarm most of the ladies present". The new development opened up the land around Preston New Road as an appealing prospect for Blackburn's middle class in trade, education, the law or working for the new Borough Corporation.

The first such houses had been built shortly after the turnpike was first opened – 'Spring-Mount' at the top of Montague Street was one example, to which millowner, lawyer, and briefly (before being unseated on petition) Blackburn's MP William Eccles moved from *Bank House* in 1839. Other buildings were the gifts of those whose mansions lay further down the road: Henry Sudell's butler, Richard Brown, used a golden handshake from his fleeing master to build the *Fox and Grapes* Inn, and Sir John Rutherford built houses for his chauffeur, valet and secretary at 108-12 Revidge Road. However, from the 1860s onwards, the Brow was swamped by the new homes of those escaping the town centre.

Villas for the well-to-do, in many ways scaled-down copies of the mansions further out of town, sprouted up alongside Preston New Road. By the start of the First World War there were nearly two hundred households, mostly those of millowners, professionals, or 'gentlemen'. The area benfited from the advent of tram travel in 1886, when a Number 22 would take passengers to Billinge End, and the arrival of telephones, most of which in Blackburn were to be found in the Billinge area. There was even the novelty of a public telephone kiosk (or

A drawing for the Illustrated London News of January 1864. The Corporation employed operatives made workless by the Cotton Famine to build Corporation Park, and the houses on the bank up to Revidge.

'*cabinet*' as these quainter constructions were called) at Billinge End crossroads. The box was watched by the police – who later established their own outpost there – after four men were discovered using the table and chairs inside to play cards!

Most sweeping of all, however, was the eradication or beseiging of most of the old farms and cottages on the Brow by the new terraces of respectable artisans' or lower-middle-class houses which now occupy the area. The names of previously familiar spots such as '*The Dingle*', '*Lob Hall*' or '*Tean Barn*' (at the top of Duke's Brow) were replaced by streets bearing the names of figures such as Queen Adelaide, consort to William IV in the 1830s, Princess Alexandra, who married the future Edward VII in 1863, or Victorian statesmen such as Granville or Cranborne. As Barbara Riding has shown in a recent study of the area for the Blackburn Local History Society's journal (1992), the terraces followed the lines of the previous field pattern, and some farm names such as '*New Bank*', and '*Higher Bank*' still survive today in street names. Even traces of the old farm buildings themselves, as well as weavers' cottages at Mile End and the top of the Brow, are still to be found with effort.

Church, School and Sport

WITH the thousands of new residents this brought to the West of Blackburn came schools, churches, recreation and trade. Since 1826 there had been a school at what is now 66, Preston New Road, established by Quaker George Edmundson, Carlyle's terse phrase,"*ca'd it an Academy*" – although it was expressly practical rather than academic. In 1834 St. Silas' (then called Billinge) Sunday School was opened at what are now the parish rooms on Preston New Road after some months' delay caused by a builders' strike. By the 1880s, however, the urgent need for more schools in the area was recognised by Blackburn's School Board. '*Edmundson's Academy*', with nearly 100 pupils, expanded to its rear into the adjoining low building now used by QEGS. The Grammar School itself, with a similar number of students, moved from its room in Freckleton Street to what were described as "*elegant premises*" costing £7,000 in West Park Road, which still form the nucleus of the school. St. Silas' School also moved at this time to its current location in Clematis Street, and Sacred Heart School was opened by the Roman Catholic Church in 1900. A number of small private schools also flourished, including one at '*All Springs*', Duke's Brow, another at No. 1 Granville Road, and a Methodist Sunday School run from 1874 onwards at '*Duke's Hall*' on Alexandra Road.

Meanwhile, a wealthy tobacconist called James Hargreaves had responded to the lack of a school for his daughter by establishing the Girls' High School himself at '*Spring Mount*' in 1883 with the help of other local notables. The number of pupils rose rapidly from 29 to 150, and in 1891 the new building still adjoining

'*Spring Mount*' was erected to accommodate them. Although a dozen industrial scholarships were available, the school's intake was chiefly from the comfortable homes around Preston New Road: those who were pupils in the early Twentieth Century remember most girls' being collected by domestic servants and ferried home by car. The High School later moved to Cross Hill, and eventually became part of Witton School.

The tradition of independent education for girls was taken up by *Westholme School* which began at (and took its name from) the home of its founder (at 167 Preston New Road), a Miss Singleton, in 1923. Starting with only eight pupils – the children of local friends who had asked her to take their charge – Principal Singleton's businesslike approach made the school thrive where other minor schools withered. She took on staff, hired rooms at the Trinity Wesleyan Church a the top of Montague Street, and by 1930 had moved on to '*Billinge House*'. For six guineas a term, Westholme offered a comparatively wide curriculum and a degree of exclusivity. In 1950 the school and assets were handed on by Miss Singleton to her successors, who expanded to '*Beardwood Bank*' in 1957, and later still occupied '*Wilmar Lodge*' amid the affluent and increasingly popular surroundings of Meins Road.

Most recently of all, John Thwaites' home at '*Troy*' became part of, and then made way for, Blakey Moor Girls' Secondary School, later Billinge, and now Beardwood School.

Where schoolchildren had their work, adults had their play, and opportunities arose for this at East Lancs Cricket Club, opened at Alexandra Meadows in 1863, (patronised famously by the Hornbys) and Blackburn Golf Club, which first rented land on Revidge Heights in 1894. For those unwilling or unable to stump up the fee for such clubs, a more leisurely time could be had over a drink in any of the pubs which had sprung up in the area: *Dog Inn, Alexandra Hotel, Leamington Hotel, West View Inn, Quarryman's Arms* and *Gibraltar Inn* have all been ready to serve you a pint since the 1890s (or longer) – although now it will cost more than the 1d. it would have then!

And if you felt like paying penance after a crawl around the local hostelries, all denominations were ready to greet you. The Anglicans had established a mission at Billinge as early as 1846, but it was thirty years before a new parish there was contemplated. Without large-scale benefactors, funds had to be raised by local – though prosperous – parishioners. The church opened in 1898, but was not consecrated until 1900, and had to wait until 1913 for its porch, baptistry and tower. Such was the tradition of appealing to parishioners for support that rented pews were not actually abolished until 1982!

The Baptists opened their grand church in Leamington Road in 1893, extending it in 1911, and not to be outdone, the Roman Catholics established a chapel-of-ease of St. Anne's at Sacred Heart School in 1900. A new parish was created in 1905, but the reluctance of local landowners to co-operate with the Catholics meant that it was not until 1937 that the foundation stone of the present church could be laid, on the former Stanley estate of the Harrison family.

Shops, too, sprang up amongst the new houses – New Bank Road was a popular site from the start, but booksellers, hairdressers, electricians and shoe repairers sought their custom in Leamington Road, Duke's Brow and Alexandra Road amongst others. The West End Garage on Preston New Road was in operation by the 1930s. Two traders in particular, however, prospered with the developments in the area, taking the saying *where there's muck, there's brass* more literally than most.

The first was Charles Lodge, who had been a horticulturist on the Gawthorpe estate in Duke's Brow until the 1870s, when he moved over Revidge to Beardwood to establish the nurseries which his family ran there for nearly a century. Lodge's Nurseries occupied the land – and the old cottage, now modernised – which lies between the foot of Beardwood Brow and Preston New Road. So successful was the enterprise that it expanded across the junction to the land still used as a garden centre. At its height, there were five greenhouses,

---

BLEGBURN FRA REVIDGE

T'windo's o' Blegburn wink i' t'westerin' sun;
An' a theawsand chimleys, like slaw scholars, try
Wi' their pencils—clumsy-like—to scrawl
Their bits o' hooamwork on to t'smudgy sky.
An' then a flush o' rose, till t'dusk cooms deawn
Wi' an incense-blue. And then a quiet pause
As Blegburn rigs itsel', as if it's beawn
Wi' strings o' costume-jects an' blazin' brooaches
Eawt to'art Preston, t'Accrin'ton or Bowton—
Ready to shaw 'em, when id day's wark's done
Id knaws just heaw a hardheyd northern teawn
Should dress for swank, an' heve it bit o' fun.

John Sparth

POETRY.

SONG OF BILLINGE HILL.

I was king of this town before Homer was born,
  The remnant am I of a mountain ;
By a tornado rude from my sire I was torn,
  And pitched close to Wagtail's weird fountain.
It caused a deep basin to make me a swell,
  Clear to all who have brains geologic ;
Far down in my caverns the fairies did dwell,
  Who spell-bound held Samlesbury by magic.

I've been buried for ages by glaciers complete,
  When there was not a biped beholder ;
And my entrails consumed, too, by subterrene heat,
  Ere the mammoth had trod on my shoulder.
I've seen races prodigious spring up and decay,
  Unsung by the Greek or the Roman ;
Many a Bathsheba's charms have I seen in my day,
  Many a Solomon sigh for a woman.

Many a gay cavalier, on his sprightliest steed,
  Here for honour and love hath done duty,
See the Briton and Roman in conflict did bleed,
  Or the world had been pledged for a " beauty."
Great Derby and Cromwell were puppets compared
  With the antediluvian heroes.
When Og, Gog, and Magog their sabres unbared,
  What a farce were your Cæsars and Neroes.

From a site so commanding what have I not seen
  In the wars with the red and white roses—
The gew-gaws of Royalty torn on the green,
  And their parasites bleeding at noses.
I've seen Charlie Stuart come snorting along
  While Proud Preston hath rung with his praises ;
But this recluse of Flora, Macdonald was flung
  Near to Derby, and lost the crown-races.

When King Jamie came down, what a treat !—how divine !—
  What a feast to the Lancashire Witches !
When he held up his sword o'er the famous sirloin
  Then my mate wore his velveteen breeches.
What a roll from the drums !—how the trumpets did blare !
  As the stag bounded o'er the green meadow ;
But when he departed Sir Richard did stare
  When the buns on the hill cast their shadow.

When the brave Prince of Orange, sweet William the Third
  Sent in exile a king broken-hearted,
And in sorrow and grief taught the " cannie " old bird
  That the " fool and his throne are soon parted "—
I felt my foundations with laughter to shake
  When Will's effigy landed at Hoghton,
For the priests had all damned him for heresy's sake,
  And the troubles their flock he had brought on.

On my apex the eagle now buildeth his nest,
  Of the birds of the air he's the sovereign ;
But in far grander plumes his ancestors were drest,
  Which of yore o'er my head I've seen hovering.
I've the wee peggy-white-throat, the puny tom-tit,
  And the wren, and the redbreast at vespers,
My orchestra the nightingale left in a " fit,"
  Still his voice oft I hear in soft whispers.

I've seen in past ages the " primitive man,"
  Near Ribchester, afloat on a rafter—
Seen the dragon spit fire, which Medea outran,
  Which St. George slew some thousands years after.
I've seen lately disturbed with some squalls I don't like,
  Which have sadly convulsed this old borough,
Burning mansions and mills—Oh, the people on strike,
  I would gibbet their leaders to-morrow.

I had shivered long ages in barrenness here
  Before my late friend, Joseph Fielding,
Had made me a fit habitation for deer,
  Which his son takes a pride now in shielding.
'Gainst " roughs," and the poachers a boundary he made,
  When they " dubbed " him the lord of the manor ;
Hoghton Tower and old Pendle were cast in the shade,
  When my saplings unfurled the green banner.

Now progress runs rampant and science outstrips
  The speed of the lathe, or the shuttle ;
Who once could have thought that bleak Billinge had lips
  And could sing to an audience so subtle ?
When the aeronaut pitches his tent in the moon,
  And the Channel is " bridged " by a bather,
Steel-piercing torpedoes have made a buffoon—
  A true Balaam's ass—of my father.
                  JOHN BARON.

Blackburn, September 16, 1878.

[handwritten: P CHRONICLE SEP 21/78]

Two tributes to the beauty of Blackburn seen from the West by local poets.

two boilerhouses, a well, a long shed and working ponies on the site. The family business served both passing trade and the families in the grand halls along Preston New Road. Fred Lodge, born at the turn of the century, found work as a young boy grinding knives at the Billinge Scar estate, also picking up butter from the adjoining farm before heading off to school every morning. Lodge's name remains familiar to Blackburn's maturer gardening buffs, even though the nurseries closed thirty years ago, and its plot has now been built over.

Florist and landscape gardener Robert Fergusson also moved to Beardwood in the late Nineteenth Century, living at 'Billinge Scar', 'Higher Toad Hole', and eventually the house standing behind the nurseries which still bear his (re-spelt) name. During the First World War, the land there was ploughed up, making it useless for the horses which had been kept there before. The plot was then put to the use for which it has been known to those in need of a garden plant or a bouquet of flowers ever since.

It was not until 1926 that Beardwood began to take on the form we see it in today. In September of that year, Daniel Thwaites' trustees passed on his extensive properties in Woodfold and Beardwood (and throughout Blackburn) to his daughter, Elma Yerburgh. Throughout the next fifty years, small parcels of land were leased, sold or even given away to allow the building of the houses now on the old farmlands. Tracts were sold to the Golf Club in 1927; to Blackburn Corporation to build the Arterial Road in 1929; and one by one, houses in West View Place or Revidge were sold to long-standing tenants, and plots granted to those wanting to build new homes at Beardwood. By the start of the Second World War, there were a dozen houses on Beardwood Brow and White Road, as many opposite Thwaites' old home at 'Beardwood Cliff' running along Preston New Road, and still more again on Wyfordby Avenue, which took its name from a Leicestershire manor owned by the Yerburgh family (now known by the title Lord Alvingham).

Cartoons drawn by workers who built Yew Tree Drive, called "The arterial road" ever since the 1920's, reflected mixed feelings about the project and their employers, even if the pay was a welcome relief from unemployment. The scheme, to take men off "the dole", was not unlike that adopted by the Corporation in the 1860's to build Corporation Park and houses on Duke's Brow.

The End of an Era

When the War ended, the old mansions were demolished, deserted or converted. 'Wycollar', 'Whinfield', and Rutherford's 'Beardwood' made way for new homes; 'Beardwood Bank', 'Troy', 'Beardwood Cliff' and 'Beardwood Hall' became schools or hospitals; and 'Billinge Scar' and *Woodfold Hall* were plundered by builders and auctioneers. The latter was stripped in May 1949, three years after the death of Mrs. Yerburgh, at a reputedly riotous three-day auction in which nearly 800 lots – including everything from white marble statues to Eighteenth-century mezzotints, carpets, antique furniture, Thwaites' library and even coffee-pots, lawn-mowers and a mahogany wheelchair —went under the hammer for buyers travelling up from London. The auctioneers left no stone unturned – but did, however, forget to empty the wine cellars, a job left to later visitors! The hall itself (which had never had electricity) did not sell, and has deteriorated ever since. A Listed building, it still stands as a sad reminder of the prosperity and power which had left Blackburn by the 1950s, taking with them the glamour which had once bedecked Beardwood and Billinge.

Piecemeal development of the roads around the West of Blackburn continued throughout the 1950s and '60s, new houses being added to those already established on Beardwood Brow, Preston New Road and Wyfordby Avenue. This process was accelerated in the 1970s and '80s with the construction of homes pouring downwards into Beardwood from Lammack, and the new motel on the Arterial Road. Once again, Blackburn's West End has new residents with new interests, and a further chapter opens in its history. All that remains of the farming and residential past of the area are occasional buildings, walls, street names, and memories. Many – but by no means all – of these are recorded here as faithfully as possible, but I'll be glad to hear of any errors and omissions – or any comments you may have!

Yew Tree Cottage, Toad Hole, as it looked for over three centuries

Flowing from Beardwood to Toad Hole, 'Arley Brook' was diverted to its present course when the turnpike was built in 1825.

Bank House, Duke's Brow and the more humble bobbin shop which stood below it until about 1853 (below).

34

No through road! The old path to Preston down Beardwood Brow and straight on couldn't cater for modern traffic.

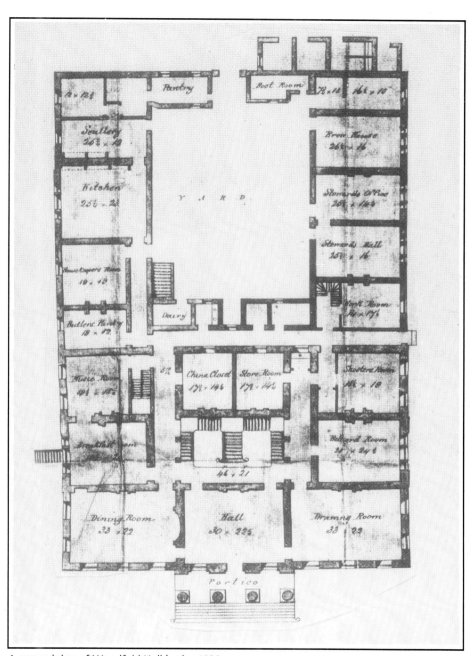

A groundplan of Woodfold Hall in the 1830s.

Top: Woodfold Hall, home of Blackburn's elite from the 1790s to the 1940s;

Middle: The orangery in Woodfold's gardens;

Bottom: Shown here at Woodfold is "Combination III" which was highly commended when exhibited by Robert Yerburgh in London in 1897.

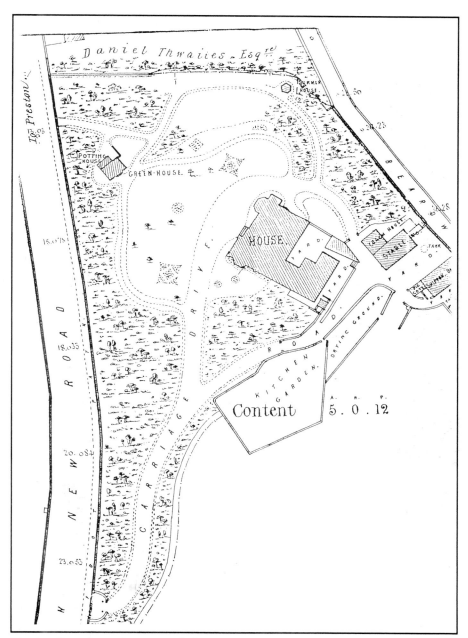

The Beardwood Mansion estate, built on the land between the old and new roads to Preston. The 5-acre site was mapped in 1886.

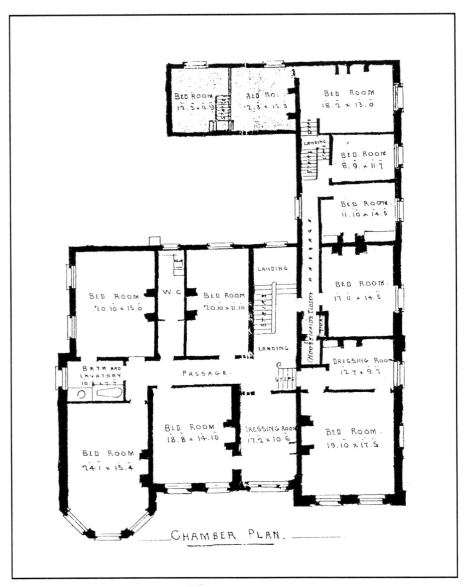

The room plans of "Beardwood Mansion", latterly the home of Sir John Rutherford M.P., as it stood in the 1880s.

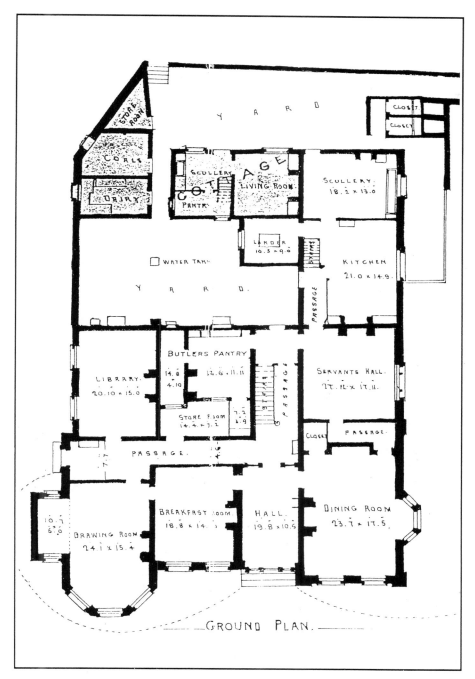

STORE ROOM

COALS

DAIRY

SCULLERY

COTTAGE

PANTR'

LIVING ROOM

SCULLERY.
18.2 × 13.0

CLOSET

CLOSET

Y A R D

WATER TANK

LARDER
10.3 × 9.0

KITCHEN
21.0 × 14.9

Y A R D.

PASSAGE

LIBRARY.
20.10 × 15.0

BUTLERS PANTRY
14.8   13.6 × 11.11
4.10

STORE ROOM
14.4 × 7.2

7.2
3.9

SERVANTS HALL.
17.11 × 17.11

CLOSET   PASSAGE.

PASSAGE

PASSAGE.

DRAWING ROOM
24.1 × 15.4

10.7
6.0

BREAKFAST ROOM
18.8 × 14.3

HALL.
19.8 × 10.6

DINING ROOM
23.7 × 17.5

GROUND PLAN.

41

In 1936, 'Beardwood Mansion' was demolished to make way for Beardwood Drive, which Rutherford used as a garage (inset). It still serves as such, though now attached to a new home.

The Shackerley Toll Bar at Yew Tree charged travellers on the turnpike for nearly half a century from 1842, and the Yew Tree Inn opposite gave them solace for nearly a century and a half.

"*Beardwood Cliff*", later '*Nazareth House*' and its extensive gardens as captured for the *Thompson family album in the 1890s.*

'Troy', the home of John and Ada Thwaites, on the site now occupied by Beardwood (formerly Billinge) School. (Photo courtesy of Robin Whalley).

'Beardwood Hall' at the turn of the century. It now serves as 'Beardwood Hospital'

The old 'Nazareth House', with its lavish interior, was demolished in 1989, leaving only the Lodge, which still overlooks Preston New Road.

46

The lodge for 'Wycollar' (centre), the Coddington family home. William Coddington was one of Blackburn's MPs from 1880 to 1906. Skilfully extended, the lodge retains its original style. 'Wycollar' itself was demolished shortly after 1930, when these photographs of the house (top and bottom) were taken.

The lodge for 'Whinfield' still stands on Preston New Road. Its occupant was in the service of Harry Hornby, Blackburn's M.P. for 23 years (1886-1910) and textile manufacturer Eli Heyworth. If the lodge is anything to go by, 'Whinfield' must have been a very fine house.

Below: East Lancs cricket team in 1880: The man out of whites is J. Fisher Armistead of 'Beardwood House'. In the background, the blurred form of the 'Alexandra Hotel' is recognisable. Several of the team were local residents, and are regarded as 'greats' by today's cricket enthusiasts. A. N. Hornby's family lived at 'Whinfield', Preston New Road.

'Billinge Scar' where the Birtwistle family lived in the style of county gentry.

BILLINGE SCARR.

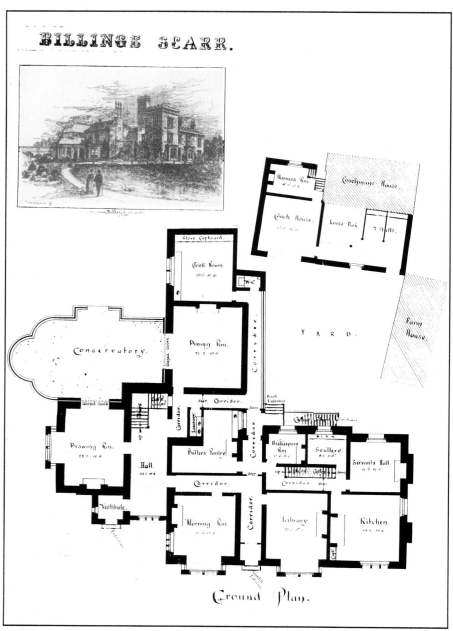

Plans of 'Billinge Scar' drawn up by the Thwaites' surveyor in 1889.

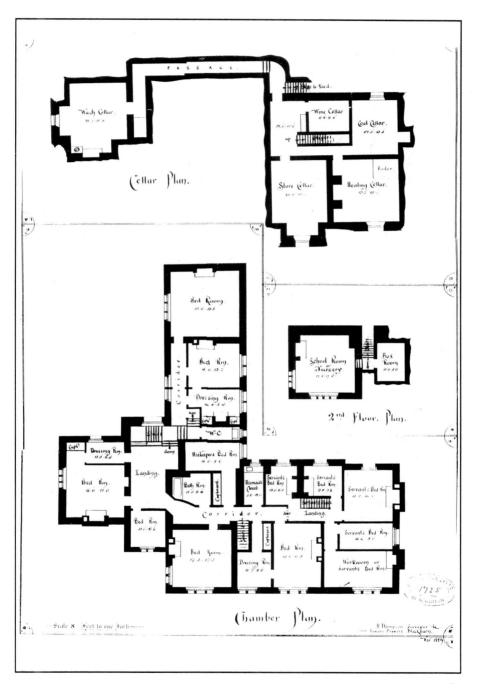

Cellar Plan.

Wash Cellar.

PASSAGE.

Wine Cellar.

Coal Cellar.

Store Cellar.

Heating Cellar.

Boiler.

Bed Room.

Bed Rm.

Dressing Rm.

School Room
or
Nursery.

Box Room.

2nd Floor. Plan.

Corridor.

W.C.

Dressing Rm.

Landing.

Bath Rm.

Hsekeepers Bed Rm.

Cupbd.

Bed Rm.

Housemaids Closet.

Servants Bed Rm.

Servants Bed Rm.

Servants Bed Rm.

Corridor.

Landing.

Cupboard.

Bed Rm.

Servants Bed Rm.

Bed Room.

Dressing Rm.

Bed Rm.

Workroom or Servants Bed Rm.

Chamber Plan.

Scale 8 Feet to one Inch

H Thompson Surveyor &c
Union Street, Blackburn.

Nov 1889

51

Billinge Scar' was said to have the largest greenhouses in Lancashire. The main one was 150 feet in length, giving the eight gardeners a head start in the horticultural competitions from which they brought back many cups and certificates.

William Birtwistle, "the man who commanded more looms than any other single individual in the world" at his home, 'Billinge Scar' after the first World War. He held the first driving licence in Blackburn in 1904 and was a very enthusiastic motorist.

The old coach house and the stone wall (a third of a mile long) are nearly all that remains of 'Billinge Scar' built by Daniel Thwaites, although a farm continues to be worked from a farmhouse alongside it.

The imposing gateway of 'Billinge Scar', no longer opens onto the elaborate ornamental gardens which fitted the lifestyle of its owners. The lower picture shows that the original gates have been re-hung on iron pillars inside the stone columns.

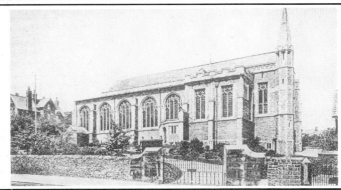

The three churches serving the newly-built homes of Duke's Brow: Leamington Road Baptist Chapel, built 1895 and extended 1911: St. Silas' C of E Church built in the 1890s, had to wait some years after this photograph was taken before acquiring its tower: Sacred Heart R.C. Church across Preston New Road from St. Silas' had its foundation stone laid in October 1937.

The conservatory and the hallway of 'Billinge Scar', as the Birtwistles knew them. The conservatory's glass ceiling had been replaced but the floor still boasted its Italian mosaic tiles.

Above and right: The cottage at Higher Toad Hole has lost its coachman's quarters, its farm buildings and its inn sign since the 18th century, although clues of their existence are still to be seen.

Below: A pair of 17th century cottages at Beardwood. The original heavy lintels on the windows and the uneven brickwork are evidence of their age and their use for weaving.

Photographs of New Bank Road and Duke's Brow in the early years of this century show how Blackburn's "leafy suburbs" were developing.

The building of private homes in the late 19th century around Duke's Brow brought with it the need to have public houses too. The 'Quarryman's Arms', 'The Dog Inn', 'The West View Inn' and 'Leamington Hotel', shown here are four such hostelries still used by local residents, as are (not shown) 'The Gibraltar Inn', and 'The Alexandra Hotel'. They supplemented existing inns 'The Yew Tree' and 'The Fox and Grapes'.

Billinge (or here called Billings) End had "all mod. cons" by about 1910, when this photo was taken, including a regular tram service and a public telephone. This was housed in a rustic cabin shown on the left of the picture. Lynwood Road, built on farm land parallel with Duke's Brow, was still incomplete in 1905 when this picture was taken. With small front gardens and spacious bay windows, these were very desirable residencies when compared with those in older streets in the town.

This 1926 aerial shot of Preston New Road shows the great mansions of Blackburn in their last days as private houses alongside the advancing streets of less spectacular homes. In the lower right corner is 'Troy' with its huge wooded garden. In the lower left corner stands 'Wycollar'. (Aerofilms Library)

JUNCTION OF ARTERIAL ROAD AND PRESTON NEW ROAD.

The arterial road, properly called 'Yew Tree Drive', seen at the time of its opening in 1928. The "Thwaites" sign stands out behind the "Yew Tree Inn" and its out-buildings. The turnpike's original setts can be seen in the road's gutter, and "The Saxon Inn" or "Moat House" will not appear for half a century.